Sh[oes]

by Fay Robinson
illustrated by Larry Moore

Harcourt

Orlando Boston Dallas Chicago San Diego

www.harcourtschool.com

2 feet and 2 feet are 4 feet.

4 shoes for you!

4 feet and 2 feet are 6 feet.

6 shoes for you!

0 feet and 0 feet is 0 feet.

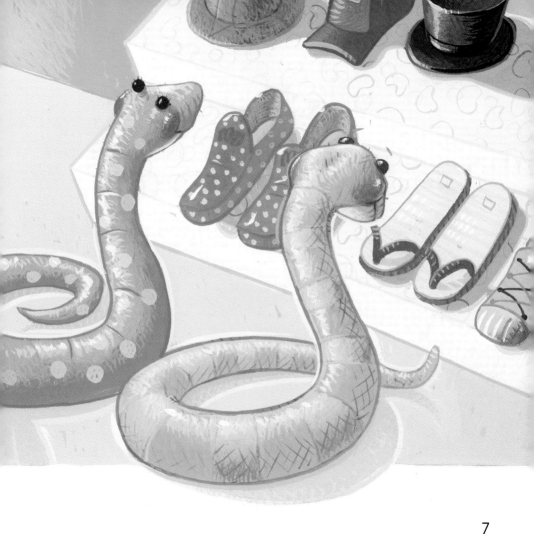

Hats for you!